CW01305706

**Demonolatry Rites**

# Demonolatry Rites
## A Collection of Ritual

Collected and Compiled by S. Connolly

**Demonolatry Rites**

# Demonolatry Rites
## A Collection of Ritual

Collected and Compiled by S. Connolly

**DB PUBLISHING**
United States of America

©Copyright 2005 and 2008 by OFS, and S. Connolly. Each individual ritual is copy written by its creator. No part of this book may be reproduced in whole or in part in any format without express written consent from the author(s).

**Demonolatry Rites**

# CONTENTS

| | |
|---|---|
| Introduction | 9 |
| A Rite to the Prince of This World - Satan (Geifodd ap Pwyll) | 11 |
| Rite to Belial (OFS) | 21 |
| Rite to Lucifer (OFS) | 25 |
| Rite to Flereous (OFS) | 29 |
| Rite to Leviathan (OFS) | 33 |
| Rite for Creating a Talisman With the Aid of a Daemon (Michael C. Brower) | 37 |
| Pillars of the Sisters (S. Connolly) | 41 |
| The Journey Meditation (H.P. Aramon) | 45 |
| The Elemental Curse (S. Connolly) | 49 |
| The Pyramid Rite of Nine For the Passage to Adepthood (S. Connolly) | 53 |
| A Standard Initiation Rite with Baptism (M. Delaney and S. Connolly) | 61 |
| A Rite to Rid Oneself of Previous Religious Dogma (J. Caven) | 67 |
| A Rite to Make a Person or Situation Leave Your Life (S. Connolly) | 69 |

A Down to Earth Love Rite to Find a Companion
(S. Connolly and S. Davies)          **71**

A Rite to Protect Your Car (S. Connolly)    **75**

Simple Home Cleansing (S. Connolly)    **77**

Dispel Negativity (S. Connolly)    **79**

Finding Lost Items (S. Connolly)    **81**

To Learn Magick (S. Connolly)    **83**

To Infuse and Item w/Demonic Energy
                                    **85**

## Appendices I.

The Nine Divinities – Considerations (S. Connolly)
                                    **87**

Diagrams of Ritual Layout    **91**

## Appendices II.

The Enns for the Dukante Hierarchy    **93**

Notes    **99**

# Introduction

Welcome to a collection of Demonolatry rites. It has been revised to include some of S. Connolly's additional rituals that use to be available in the once "in publication" book, *The Complete Book of Demonolatry Magic*. Some of the rituals were chosen for their beauty and heartfelt creation. Others were selected because of their effectiveness. A huge debt of gratitude goes out to the priests, priestesses, initiates and adepts who created and performed these rites then offered them for publication so that other Demonolators may enjoy them.

You will notice a wide variety of rites, some in the traditions of traditional demonolatry, and others that meander from the ordinary. The variety of the rites explores a wide range of beliefs and practices to ensure that every Demonolator can find something of worth within this book.

Also included is a handy reference in the back of the book that will make it easier for you to modify any of the existing rites for personal use, and will provide more information about the Nine Divinities, Invocation and Enns.

It is my hope that you enjoy reading and performing these rites as much as I did. May the blessings of the demons be with you always.

~S. Connolly, Editor

## A Rite To The Prince Of This World (Satan)
*By Geifodd ap Pwyll*

The following ritual is designed to be performed outdoors, preferably in a woodsy area, right at twilight. It is important that the participants take their time; this procedure should not be rushed. Ideally, this rite is intended for group participation; however, it works just as well in a solitary context. Any readers who want to practice it in such a context will be required to make adjustments to the litany accordingly.

Frequently, Satanic rituals involve the use of altars, athames, incense, etc. They also usually include invocations to the four elements. This ritual is notably different in that it does not require either of these things. In the context of this rite, the earth itself serves as your altar, and conjuration of the elements is considered unnecessary.

When you go out into a woodsy area to perform this rite, first spend some time to find a particular place that just "feels right" to you. Take particular notice of how the arrangement of the trees effects you; you may want to pick an area with lots of overhanging branches. Or, you may want to pick an area in which the sky will be exposed. Dress simply but respectfully; ceremonial attire is not necessary (nor is it discouraged), but no T-shirts with any silly pictures or slogans on them, please. The color of your wardrobe should be black, or some dark "earthy" color (e.g., dark green, dark brown, etc.).

When an appropriate woodsy area has been located, and everyone is assembled for ritual, all participants must stand in a circle so that they are facing each other. Everyone begins the ritual with a customary moment of silence. Then, everyone raises their hands in the sign of the horns. With their left hands, everyone will draw a point-down pentagram in the air before them, at eye-level. Everyone keeps their hands upraised as the celebrant recites the following:

*At this, the time when the sun descends
And the brilliance of heaven is made to end;
When barrier of daylight is made to die
And an entrance is made of the nighttime sky;*

*We call forth to the One who rules this Earth,
The Trickster who laughs and is full of mirth;
Cloven hoof'd Spirit and Demon of Light
Angel of Darkness and King of the Night!*

Now all participants must join hands and move slowly in a circular formation, counter-clockwise. It may be necessary to practice doing this before commencing the ritual, for the sake of avoiding collisions. (If this is a solitary ritual, then walk slowly, counter-clockwise, in a circle by yourself.) While doing this, the celebrant recites the following:

*You whose sign is the five-pointed star*
*Encasing the Goat of Mendes afar,*
*Surrounded by coil of the Dragon blamed,*
*All together address'd by Moorish name.*

*Come forth from the pit, come forth from the sky*
*Come forth from the ends of the Earth, come nigh!*
*O mighty Horned God of moonlight glow,*
*Come forth from above and come forth from below!*

**Everyone then chants:**

SATANASATANASATANASATANASATANA
SATANASATANASATANASATANAS!

**Celebrant then recites:**

*You who disrupt Eden's ignorant bliss*
*With temptation and taste of Serpent's kiss;*

*Lover of witches and friend to the dead*
*Shimmering shadow, bedazzling red.*

*Come forth from the pit, come forth from the sky*
*Come forth from the ends of the Earth, come nigh!*
*O mighty Horned God of moonlight glow,*
*Come forth from above and come forth from below!*

**Everyone:**

*SATANASATANASATANASATANASATANA SATANASATANASATANASATANAS!*

**Celebrant:**

*You who explore with horns upraised,*
*That change and becoming should always be praised;*
*Scapegoat condemned to roam desert sands*
*Honorable Traveler of foreign lands.*

*Come forth from the pit, come forth from the sky*
*Come forth from the ends of the Earth, come nigh!*
*O mighty Horned God of moonlight glow,*
*Come forth from above and come forth from below!*

**Everyone:**

*SATANASATANASATANASATANASATANA SATANASATANASATANASATANAS!*

    Everyone gets down on one knee, with their hands still joined. They will then close their eyes and remain silent for several moments. Then, while everyone's eyes are still closed, the celebrant recites the following:

*Hail, Master!*

*We invoke the blessing of Hades divine*
*For all of our loved ones and family lines.*
*Grant them the power to overcome all,*

*That they will stand straight, unburdened and tall!*

**Everyone:**

*SATANASATANASATANASATANASATANA
SATANASATANASATANASATANAS!*

**Celebrant:**

*We invoke the fire of Hell so hot
To wipe out our enemies, and their lot.
Put them in the place of destruction and waste,
That Abaddon may feast and enjoy their taste!*

**Everyone:**

*SATANASATANASATANASATANASATANA
SATANASATANASATANASATANAS!*

**Celebrant:**

*We invoke the strength of the mighty Beast
To keep us looking with hope to the east;*

*That we may excel in all of our feats
And never be made to accept defeat!*

**Everyone:**

*SATANASATANASATANASATANASATANASAT ANASATANASATANASATANAS!*

**Celebrant:**

*We invoke the Will of the Ancient Snake
To guide us and lead us, for Hell's sake
That all of our actions and all of our minds
Will serve to achieve our Master's designs!*

**Everyone:**

*SATANASATANASATANASATANASATANA SATANASATANASATANASATANAS!*

Now each participant will take turns voicing whatever prayers and/or requests they might individually have for Satan. This will begin with the person to the right of the celebrant, and it will move counter-clockwise through the circle. The celebrant will be the very last person to voice his/her prayers/requests. There should be a moment of silence between each participant's prayer/request.

When the celebrant has completed his/her own prayer/request, all participants rise back to their feet. Everyone's hands should still be joined.

**Celebrant:**

*All honor and thanks unto the Dark One,*
*For His moon has eclipsed the charlatan sun!*
*The stars are right; in honor we pray,*
*For the Season of the Witch is here to stay!*

**Everyone:**

*SATANASATANASATANASATANASATANA SATANASATANASATANASATANAS!*

All participants once again raise their arms in the sign of the horns. They trace pentagrams in the air before them with their left hands, and together they recite the following:

*Hail, Satan! Hail, Satan! Hail, Satan! AMEN!*

All participants shake hands with each other. Once they are done, the ritual is completed.

## Rite to Belial
*Contributed by Ordo Flammeus Serpens*

Construct the elemental circle with candles in bowls of heavy earth. Upon the altar shall be placed a burner with sand and salt that water may birth the soil new life. Behold the dagger of Earth as is shall be used to invoke our Lords, and finally Lord Belial who shall preside at this rite, a ceremony in his honor. Once Lord Belial has joined us we may choose to invite other Daemons from the Earth; Ronwe, Eurynomous, Baalberith, Babael and others. The altar, facing North, shall be covered in fine powder that the daemons may trace their messages and symbols. Burn patchouli for the ritual chamber.

**To Invoke Earth**: Lirach Tasa Vefa Wehlic, Belial.

**To Invoke Air**: Renich Tasa Uberaca Biasa Icar, Lucifer.

**To Invoke Fire**: Ganic Tasa fubin, Flereous.

**To Invoke Water**: Jedan Tasa hoet naca, Leviathan.

**HP opens the ritual with**:

*Hail to the season of muted earth in all of its desolate glory - death. Bold and mounded, solid and buried. Hail our Lord Belial.*

**Sect:**

*Hail Belial!*

**Priest(ess):**

*This season births from death all new beginnings, our Lady Unsere of life. Let us pray:*

**Prayer of Devotion (said by all):**

*Hear us, O Belial of Earth. I waken you, behold. Invited to this rite we ask thee to consecrate all that stands before you. We ask you to share all that we may know all that is mundane, and of earthly pleasures. This we pray, Master of Earth. Hail Lord Belial!*

    All members of the sect may burn their requests of all earthly things; prosperity, knowledge, pleasure, and beginnings. Behold the rites of Belphegore if prosperity is your objective. Instead, pray to Lord Belial and spend time before the altar in devotion. Belial shall make his presence known in stolid, firm, heavy energy mute and in shades of earth.

**Demonolatry Rites**

# Rite to Lucifer
*Contributed By Ordo Flammeus Serpens*

The Altar shall face the East. All tapers should be colored white, yellow, and pink. Incense made of Lemon and sandalwood shall be burnt at all elemental points. Behold the dagger of air by which all of the elementals shall be invoked starting with Lucifer. Softly, in the background, *Meleus de quo Magna*.

**To Invoke Air**: Renich Tasa Uberaca Biasa Icar, Lucifer.

**To Invoke Fire**: Ganic Tasa fubin, Flereous.

**To Invoke Water**: Jedan Tasa hoet naca, Leviathan.

**To Invoke Earth**: Lirach Tasa Vefa Wehlic, Belial.

**The HP Opens With:**

Lucifer brings us enlightenment and wisdom. He is the daemon of air, the light bringer.

Hail the season of wisdom, rebirth, and enlightenment. Hail to our Lord Lucifer.

**Sect:**

Hail Lucifer!

**High Priest(ess):**

Show us truth and reason. It is our Lord Lucifer who hath brought us from the darkness into the light. His winds carry with them the lessons for this lifetime.

All Hail Lucifer, Lord of Light!

**Sect:**

*Hail Lucifer!*

Invite other daemons of air be present in Lucifuge Rofocale, Verrine, and others. Prayer and meditation is appropriate for this rite. Requests may be burnt for matters of knowledge and learning, and to see that which is hidden.

## Demonolatry Rites

## Rite to Flereous
*Contributed by Ordo Flammeus Serpens*

The Altar shall face the South. All tapers should be colored orange, or red. Incense made of devil's claw, hibiscus, and red sandalwood shall be burnt at all elemental points. Behold the dagger of fire by which all of the elementals shall be invoked starting with Flereous.

**To Invoke Fire**: Ganic Tasa fubin, Flereous.

**To Invoke Water**: Jedan Tasa hoet naca, Leviathan.

***To Invoke Earth***: Lirach Tasa Vefa Wehlic, Belial.

**To Invoke Air**: Renich Tasa Uberaca Biasa Icar, Lucifer.

**High Priest(ess):**

*All Hail our Lord Flereous.*

**Sect:**

*Hail Flereous!*

**High Priest(ess):**

*We pray humbly before you, Flereous, bring us swift action, passion, and love. All hail fire for He is the third element.*

**Sect:**

*Hail Fire!*

**Priest(ess):**

*Flereous who is son of Satan, who was fire before him. We are and ever shall be a burning ember within the fire that is a part of the whole of our creation.*

**Sect:**

*Hail Flereous!*

**Priest(ess):**

*The Fire Rebirths us and as the Phoenix, we too, shall rise. Flereous commands it so. He blesses us with passion and love – for all these things are of him. Hail Flereous, Lord of Fire.*

**Sect:**

*Hail Flereous!*

The ritual proceeds with silent prayer, the burning of requests, and the sharing of the wine.

# Demonolatry Rites

# Rite To Leviathan
*Contributed by Ordo Flammeus Serpens*

The Altar shall face the West. All tapers should be colored gray or blue. Incense made of calamus or lily should be used. Bowls or cups of water shall be put at each of the elemental points. Behold the dagger of water by which all of the elementals shall be invoked starting with Leviathan. Softly, in the background, *Rite to Leviathan*.

**To Invoke Water**: Jedan Tasa hoet naca, Leviathan.

***To Invoke Earth***: *Lirach Tasa Vefa Wehlic, Belial.*

**To Invoke Air**: Renich Tasa Uberaca Biasa Icar, Lucifer.

**To Invoke Fire**: Ganic Tasa fubin, Flereous.

The elemental circle is also blessed with water and salt *"Talot pasa oida Belial et Leviathan"*

**High Priest(ess):**

*Hail our Serpent Lord, Leviathan of Water.*

*Sect:*

*Hail Leviathan!*

**High Priest(ess):**

*Hail Oroborus of eternal wisdom.*

**Sect:**

*Hail Oroborus!*

**High Priest(ess)**

*Hail Dagon of passion.*

**Sect:**

*Hail Dagon!*

**High Priest(ess)**

*For the serpent brings us strength in our emotion and design. As the tides ebb and flow, so shall the knowledge wash over us and our dominion. Bless us, Leviathan. Grant us wisdom, insight, empathy, fertility in mind, body, and spirit, and the knowledge of these mysteries. So be it, as it ever shall be. Blessed by Nemah, All Hail Leviathan.*

**Sect:**

*Hail Leviathan.*

The ritual proceeds with silent prayer, the burning of requests, and the sharing of wine.

**Demonolatry Rites**

## Rite for Creating a Talisman With the Aid of a Daemon

*Contributed by Michael C. Brower*

Aside from the basic arsenal of ritual accoutrements, you fill need to acquire a small circular or square piece of unused parchment.

### The Rite

Cast your Elemental Circle as you normally would, inviting Satan from the center.

After the Circle has been properly cast, return to your altar or worktable, and inscribe upon the parchment using your pen of art, the sigil of the daemon whose aid you seek.

On the reverse side, draw a small representation of your request or the desire you wish to have fulfilled.

This drawing need not be elaborate. It can be as crude or complex as you feel to be necessary.

Employ the enn of the particular daemon or if no enn exists, invite the daemon using a summons of your own design.

To activate and charge the talisman, allowing the daemon to exert its influence, you will use your own life force.

Draw blood from your usual area and allow a drop or two to fall upon the talisman. Rub the blood over the talisman as you envision the fulfillment of your request.

Close the Rite as usual, thanking the daemons for their aid and attendance.

Keep the talisman in a dark cool place until the ninth night, when you will recharge it using the same procedure.

After you feel the request has been fulfilled, commit the talisman to the flames while again offering thanks to the daemon whose aid was granted.

**Demonolatry Rites**

## *Pillars of the Sisters*
*Contributed by S. Connolly*

(7 Day Ritual)

Unsere – Pillar of the Mother (Creative Force)
Delepitore – Pillar of Magick
Ashtaroth – Pillar of Love
Verrier – Pillar of Knowledge
Tezrian – Pillar of Destruction
Sonnillion – The Pillar of Strength
Asafoetida – The Pillar of Emotion

Other Feminine Demons for Consideration:
Astarte
Azlyn
Lilith

Rashoon
Taroon

**Tools:**
One Amulet for each Pillar (a disk with the sigil of the Demoness represented)

Feel free to use oleums or incenses of your choice, or not at all. The original rite I received called for neither. For my personal Rite, I actually replaced Asafoetida with Azlyn, and I've replaced Verrier with Lilith once or twice. So feel free to modify according to your own needs.

You will need a ritual space free from contamination where you can leave the amulets and energy undisturbed! For a consecutive 7 days do the following rite at the SAME time each day.

Do NOT construct an elementally balanced space. Instead, place the Seven Amulets in a circular fashion in the center of the room (leaving about 1-2 feet between each one on all sides). Invoke each of the sisters via their Enns. As you recite the Enn, imagine a pillar rising from the amulet on the ground and lifting through the ceiling of the room (or going up into the sky if your ritual space is outdoors). Meditate on each pillar, giving it color, texture, and form. Infuse it with the energy for its particular purpose. Do NOT dismiss the Demonic energy with a standard, "Thank you and go in peace". Leave it be.

On the seventh night, after you've done your visualization and invocation on each pillar, step inside the circle of amulets, feeling the energy from all the pillars surround you. Raise your arms above you with outstretched hands and recite the following seven times (you can modify this prayer to your liking or write your own):

"I am as Tezrian going into battle, and Sonnellion, in control of all before me. I am as Unsere, the wise matriarch, and Delepitore, the High Priestess. In the names of Ashtaroth, Verrier, and Asafoetida, I ask you grant me emotional strength to overcome my present obstacles and to emerge unscathed. Unsere, give me strength. Sonnellion, give me strength. Tezrian, give me strength. By Delepitore and the pillars of the sisters, rises the ether of all that is above me. I am the creator, the sorceress, of all before me. I am. Amen."

At the end of the final ritual, thank each Demoness present. Pick up the amulets and keep them in a safe place.

Depending on need, you can carry these amulets with you during corresponding situations. For example, carry the Amulet for Unsere into a situation that requires wisdom, or carry Tezrian into an argument. Once all of the amulets have been discharged, you can repeat the Rite to recharge them, and yourself.

**Notes:** Some people have modified this rite to do a Pillar of Brothers, or Pillar of Destruction, or Pillar of [Insert your own purpose here] rituals done in much the same way. You're basically infusing yourself and the talismans with the power of the pillars over seven days (or more or less). It's like creating a massive thought form. You can increase or decrease the number of pillars you're working with, too. There doesn't have to be just seven of them. The reason behind doing the rite the same number of days as pillars is to make sure each pillar gets equal attention

## The Journey Meditation
*Contributed by High Priest Aramon*

This ritual is one which utilizes creative visualization and is used to peer into the subconscious mind. It does not require much of anything to setup whatsoever. I do recommend soft light as you should write down what you have experienced in a journal. The more you perform this one, the more you will see.

You will need to wear comfortable loose fitting clothing or the bare minimum if you prefer. You can invoke the demons or a specific demon- your patron would be a good choice. This however, is not necessary. You can also add some soothing music. Pachelbel's "The Canon" is great for this. Any heavy music will ruin the effect.

Lay down and begin with tensing your entire body and slowly relaxing. Begin rhythmic breathing. I use a 3-5-3 pattern some of the time. The breathing pattern is optional and you should experiment with it to see if you prefer that over regular breathing.

See yourself standing in a garden. There are flowers, trees and shrubbery all around. The garden is rather large and open. To one side is a path leading up to a mountain pass. The air surrounding you is warm and comforting. Envision yourself walking up the path to the pass.

The trail rises gently to your destination. After completing your walk on the trail, you stand before the entrance to a cave. Enter and see yourself in a large chamber lit by soft light. your are the top of a staircase leading downward. Look around and take note of what you see. This you will write down in a journal afterward.

Take in as much detail as you are able to remember. This done, walk down the stairs to the main floor of the chamber. Look to your left and right. You see a mirror. Look into it. Note what you see. See every detail. Note this in your journal. Look toward the opposite wall and envision a doorway. Walk toward it and enter. This hallway leads to the outside. See yourself walk to the other end and exit the tunnel.

You should now see yourself standing in a second garden. Look around and take note of the details. Write this in your journal afterward. As you look around you will see the garden is at the edge of a cliff. Allow yourself to hear the waves of the ocean below. Walk toward it. As you arrive, you will see a trail leading back to the first garden. When you are ready, walk the trail back to the starting point.

This is the end of the ritual. Take as much time as you need for this exercise. This one is most often done with two people. I find, however, it is more often better to perform solo. Make sure you remember as much as you can from the entire session. Write down everything you can remember- highlighting those parts I have noted in the text.

## Demonolatry Rites

# The Elemental Curse
*Contributed by S. Connolly*

In place of the elementals invoke:

- Eurynomous – North
- Tezrian – East
- Amducious – South
- Sonnillion – West
- Satan – Center

Use purple and white candles to project as black candles will absorb negativity. Anoint with Creolin.

Carve the victim's name into each candle used along with each Demon's Name and sigil.

On five sheets of parchment write the victim's name in black ink. In red ink, place demonic sigils of the five respective demons over the name of the victim on each of the five pieces of parchment. (*One demon per parchment.*)

Put one drop of your own blood on each piece of parchment. Take each piece of paper to its respective direction.

Say over each: **"Vengeance be mine by death in the name of [Demon]."**

Burn the parchment in the candle flame. Place in the offering bowl. Let all of the candles burn down and place their remnants in the offering bowl.

Use a dagger to stir in black poppy and mustard seeds. Add one cup of graveyard dirt. Take this outside and dig a grave. Pour the contents of the offering bowl into the grave while saying:

**"We commit the body of [victim] to the ground!"**

Cover the grave with dirt and a piece of wood. (Covered grave may be stabbed with dagger.) With black paint, put the sigils of all five demons on the wood. Leave the grave for at least one month undisturbed. Do not plant anything in the soil there for a year.

Return to the ritual chamber and close the rite.

# The Pyramid Rite of Nine For The Passage To Adepthood

*Contributed by S. Connolly*

This rite can replace or compliment the first or second rites to Leviathan.

The altar, ideally, faces east or west (*use only if doing this rite in conjunction with Rite to Leviathan or else use east*). On the altar place one main pillar candle and place the other two pillars at the southwest and northwest corners of the ritual chamber (*if altar is facing east. If altar is facing west the two pillars stand in the northeast and southeast corners*). These pillars shall be deep blue or black in color.

Because this rite was performed during Rite to Leviathan, we began with

Belial, Leviathan, and Verrine. If you are invoking from the east, start with Lucifer, Amducious, and Unsere.

**From the altar invoke**:
- Belial
- Leviathan
- Verrine

**Travel clockwise to the next pillar and invoke:**
- Lucifer
- Amducious
- Unsere

**At the final pillar invoke:**
- Flereous
- Eurynomous
- Satan

**Diagram of Altar Facing West**

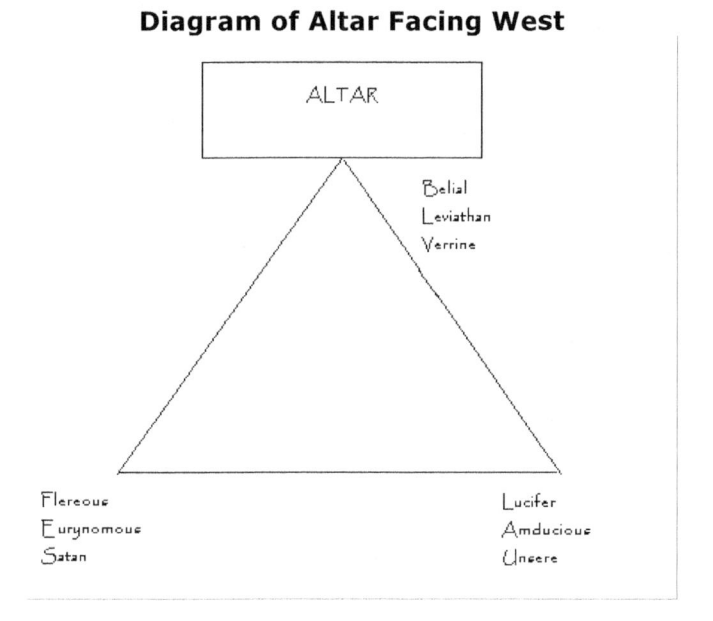

```
         ┌─────────────────┐
         │      ALTAR      │
         └─────────────────┘
                 /\
                /  \  Belial
               /    \ Leviathan
              /      \Verrine
             /        \
            /          \
           /            \
          /              \
         /                \
        /                  \
       /_____\
Flereous                   Lucifer
Eurynomous                 Amducious
Satan                      Unsere
```

Before the rite have the new adept create a 8 ½ by 11 sigil of his/her Matron/Patron. Place this on the ground in the center of the triangle. The new adept is led into the triangle by the sponsoring sect adept appointed to him/her.

**High Priest:** *Step forward [new adept's name].*

**The new adept will step forward to stand upon the sigil.**

**High Priestess:** *"What is your name?"*

**Adept:** *[Gives birth name]*

**High Priestess:** *"What is it you seek?"*

**Adept:** *"Passage into Adepthood."*

**High Priest:** *"Who among you will vouch for [new adept's name]?"*

**Sponsoring Adept:** *"I, [name], believe (s)he is ready to take this vow."*

**High Priest** (to new adept): *"Will you, [name], take this vow into this new phase of your life?"*

**Adept:** *"Yes."*

**High Priest:** *"Do any of you present object?"*

Upon no objections, **High Priest:** *"Then take your vow."*

*Vow may be memorized or read from a prewritten piece of paper.*

**Adept:** *I [demonic name] vow to uphold the courtesies, to respect the demons I work with, and to hold sacred the enns, the rites, and the wisdom the demons show unto me. Before all present, and in witness of the nine divinities, I profess my faith and responsibility to myself. A new door has opened for me. May I step through?"*

**High Priestess**: *"Welcome Adept [demonic name]. Our brother/sister emerges from the darkness blessed. Bathed in the Light of Lucifer. Please kneel."*

**The adept kneels before the priestess, with the sigil of his/her Matron/Patron beneath him/her.**

**The priestess takes the sword and puts it (flat side down) on the adept's right shoulder.** *"By [adept's Matron/Patron] may your path be lit with wisdom and love.* (Touches sword flat side down to left shoulder) *By Satan I hereby proclaim you Adept. Rise. Answer one last question before I allow you to leave your* *years of initiate training behind you. What is the all?"*

**Adept:** *"The all is one. His name is Satan."*

**Priest and Priestess:** *"Hail Satan!"*

**Entire Sect:** *"Hail Satan!"*

The priest and priestess step aside from the altar so that the adept may approach it. The Adept picks up the sigil of his/her Matron/Patron and approaches the altar. Upon the drawing of his/her blood, (s)he places several drops on the sigil and burns it in the offering bowl.

The wine is drunk in celebration and the rite is ended moving counterclockwise and thanking each of the nine divinities at the appropriate point of origin.

**Concerning Demonic Names:**
The Demonic Name is the name the demons give the adept (via a divination session done prior to the rite) before the adepthood rite. The use of the birth name at the beginning of the rite and demonic name at the end of the rite is symbolic of the passage.

## Modifications:

While this rite was written for the sect who has both a priest and priestess presiding, the script for the priest(ess) can be changed to all Priest or all Priestess as necessary.

This rite cannot and should not be performed solitary, but with modification and the guidance of a recognized and officially ordained (i.e. ordained in the flesh by another member of the traditional priesthood) member of the traditional priesthood it can be considered a legitimate passage to adepthood.

## *Please Read This Important Note*

*Do not be alarmed at the erratic energy flow during this rite. The construct of a pyramid is much different from the even flow of a circle. Some sect members may feel invigorated and others drained. Some will find they feel uncomfortable or agitated. This is perfectly normal for a nine rite of this nature.*

**Demonolatry Rites**

## A Standard Initiation Rite With Baptism
*Contributed by M. Delaney and S. Connolly*

This rite may be done during Rite to Flereous or First Rite to Leviathan. Initiates must be a minimum of 18 years of age.

Prior to the Rite the Priest must arrange to have the initiate's Matron/Patron sigil tattooed, cut, or branded onto the initiate after the Rite if the initiate's dedication did not already include that step.

The Elemental or Nine Circle is cast (do not use triangle) as usual. The usual rite may be performed before or after the initiation. The initiate is blind-folded and brought to the ritual chamber to stand outside the circle at the east-most point with an adept on either side of him/her to guide her when the time comes.

**Priest:**

*It is customary within our tradition to initiate on this day. To this altar the initiate shall come, willing and ready to acknowledge him/herself as a part of Satan. A part of the whole. From this night forward, the initiate will come to be known as [title]. We are kindred. By entering this sect this initiate becomes our brother/sister, bound in blood and by his/her dedication to [matron/patron]. It is in the grace of the nine divinities that (s)he shall enter here. So now come forth from the East, which is Lucifer, to guide you on this path. Hail Satan.*

**Sect:**

*Hail Satan.*

**The Initiate** is brought forth to stand in front of **the Priest**.

**Priest:**

*Who are you who wishes to enter this path and this sect?*

**Initiate:**

*[Gives name]*

**Priest:**

*Who is your dedicated (M)Patron?*

**Initiate:**

*[Gives Patron/Matron]*

**Priest:**

*Are you here of your own free will?*

**Initiate:**

*Yes.*

**The Blindfold is removed.**

**Priest:**

*Take your oath.*

As oaths are different in each sect the oath is now read from the parchment by the initiate. **A sample oath is as follows:**

*"I, [name], do hereby swear to abide the courtesies. I promise to respect the demons and to respect my Matron/Patron. I swear to keep secret the identities of my fellow sect members and the sect traditions, practices, and secrets shared with me. I swear my allegiance to Satan and to my brothers and sisters of this sect."*

**The initiate** will then sign the oath, place one drop of his/her blood on the parchment, fold it into small pieces, and burn it in the offering bowl.

**The initiate** then must bare his/her left should, left thigh, or the place on the body where the permanent symbol will be placed and **the Priest** will use an oleum of sorcery or dragon's blood to paint the Matron/Patron sigil on that spot. The gifts of initiation can then be given. This gift can either be a group pendant, a prayer cord, oleums, or a blank grimoire or group prayer book.

**Priest:**

> *Please kneel.*

**Initiate kneels.**

**Priest** anoints the initiate with ritual oleums then picks up the ritual sword, touching the flat edge of the blade to each shoulder as the words are spoken:

> *You are anointed, baptized, and initiated. Now stand.*

**Initiate stands** and faces the sect.

**Priest:**

> *You are now a demonolator of [sect name]. Welcome our new brother/sister.*

One by one the **sect members** will approach the initiate and shake their hand to welcome him/her. (Hugging is perfectly acceptable).

Once all members have greeted the new member the **Priest says**:

> *[Name], upon the close of this Rite you will exit to the North, with*

*Belial. For it is a new beginning. So it is done. Hail Satan.*

**Sect and Initiate:**

*Hail Satan.*

The ritual always ends with the sharing of the sacramental wine and the close of the circle. If the Rite to Leviathan or Flereous is done before, the Rite closes directly after this. If the Rite is yet to be completed the initiate stands with the rest of the sect for completion of the Rite and then exits from the North once the Rite is closed.

## A Rite To Rid Oneself of Previous Religious Dogma
*Contributed by J. Caven*

This is a ritual to rid oneself of previous religious dogma, guilt, etc. for anyone having difficulty leaving their previous religion behind.

**Needs:**
- Items symbolizing previous religious system such as crosses, stars of David, etc.

Open the circle with 4 of the demons you feel close to. They do not have to be the elementals.

From the center call your patron demon as well as Satan.

Once the circle is opened, put the items you have acquired from your previous belief system upon the altar. If you do not have those things you can draw a picture of whatever signifies your previous religion.

On a piece of parchment write the reason you are leaving the previous belief and renounce it. (This is all symbolic; one does not have to "sell their soul" to Satan)

On a different parchment write down why you have chosen to be with Satan, with your patron/matron, etc. Sign both parchments in ink made with a few drops of your own blood.

At this point you may drink a chalice of wine, as a "celebration" of your freedom from the bonds that once tied you to your previous belief.

Now burn both parchments in an offering bowl. After the rite you may either bury the ashes, or spread them to the wind.

Before closing the rite, meditate on your new path free of past luggage, thank the demons for coming, and close the circle.

# A Rite To Make a Person or Situation Leave Your Life

*Contributed by S. Connolly*

Needs:
- One 9x9 tile made of ceramic or plastic.
- Water
- One large bowl of salt.
- Chalk or grease marker
- Sage incense

Once inside your ritual circle clear a spot on your altar. Place a clean tile at the altar's center. Using your chalk or grease marker, write the person's name or the situation at the top of the tile. In the lower left corner place the sigil of Eurynomous in plea for change and in the right corner place the sigil of Leviathan to release any emotional bonds. Light a black candle on either side of the tile.

In salt, draw the following sigil and carefully place four droplets of water beneath it. It will look like this:

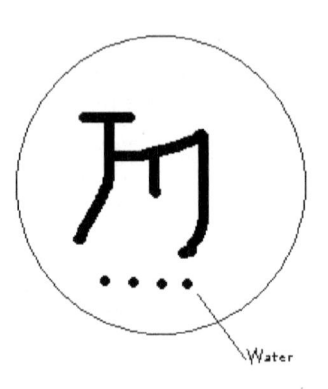

Burn the sage incense right above the sigil in a burner letting the smoke cover the sigil. Will the person, people, or situation to leave your life in the name of Eurynomous and Leviathan.

Use the ritual dagger to draw the invocation symbol in the air above the tile invoking (via enn) both Eurynomous and Leviathan.

When the rite is finished, close the ritual circle and wipe the tile clean.

## A Down to Earth Love Rite to Find a Companion

*Contributed by S. Connolly and S. Davies*

Needs:
- Red thread
- A hook in the ceiling above the altar
- A square of red cloth
- Two red candles inscribed with the sigil of Rosier.
- Sugar
- Parchment
- Red ink with a drop or two of your own blood.
- Oleums of Rosier and Belial

During this rite you must be nude. Make sure your ritual space is at a comfortable temperature.

Construct the standard elemental or Nine circle. Write the following on a piece of parchment:

## *Ponrum Ang Ronko*

Then, on the parchment also list the qualities you are looking for in a mate and anoint with both oleums. Using the ritual dagger, invoke both Rosier and Belial in the air above the parchment.

From the ceiling tie one end of the red thread to the hook in the ceiling. Bring the thread down to the altar and tie the parchment to the red candles at the base, binding the whole together. Light the candles and sprinkle them with sugar while chanting:

## *Sanm Geana Wehlc*

Infuse your own energy with the candles through prayer and meditation. Say prayers to Rosier and Belial until the candles have burned down to the parchment. Extinguish the candles and wrap the parchment and remainder of the candles in the red cloth binding it with the red thread while invoking Satan using His enn. Anoint the bag with both oleums.

Close the rite thanking all the demons invoked and keep the cloth bundle near you while you sleep for six months and you will dream of your companion.

Once your companion comes to you, go back to your ritual chamber and open the ritual circle. You must be nude once again. Unbind the contents of the cloth. Burn the remainder of the candles all the way down and burn the parchment in the offering bowl while thanking Belial and Eurynomous. Use the red cloth and red thread to make a small bag. In it, keep a rose quartz crystal anointed with oleum of Rosier. Place the bag with the crystal in the bedroom you both share.

## Demonolatry Rites

## A Rite to Protect Your Car

*Contributed by S.Connolly*

### Make an incense of equal parts
- Sandalwood
- Hibiscus
- Wormwood
- Frankincense
- Myrrh

Construct the ritual circle around the car, invoking the elementals at their respective points of origin and Satan from the center. Place the incense burner on the hood of the car and light the incense.

Circle the car three times clockwise.

Each time you approach the South most point say once:

## *Lanar Hesa Ra Satan*

Combine the salt and water and sprinkle it over the vehicle while imagining the a barrier around your vehicle.

Circle the car with the incense.

Close the rite by thanking all the demons present. Place the sigil of Satan in the glove box.

# A Simple Home Cleansing

*Contributed by S.Connolly*

This is a simple rite meant to bless your home, clear out stale and unwanted energies, and to inspire creative thinking.

On a warm day - open all the windows. Burn Sandalwood incense and candles with light scents.

Invoke the Daemon of your choice in each room.

**Demonolatry Rites**

## Dispel Negativity

*Contributed by S.Connolly*

You can work with any demon you wish.

Before the ritual, write down all of the negative things you want to expel from your life. It could be a stressful job, a bad relationship, a bad habit, a negative thinking pattern, etc...

Take 1 black candle and write all of these things onto the surface of the candle. Anoint the candle with Oleum of your choice or none at all.

Within the ritual circle, charge the candle with all the anger, sadness, jealousy, etc... you feel regarding these situations, people, or things. Light the candle and imagine yourself filled with a white light so that none of these things can affect you. Burn the piece of paper. Close the rite, but let the candle continue to burn down to nothing.

**Tip:** Try doing this rite first thing in the morning, or about mid-day.

## Finding Lost Items

*Contributed by S.Connolly*

Within a constructed ritual circle, meditate to Leviathan for help in finding a lost item. Draw the item, or write what the item was on a piece of parchment and burn it in the offering bowl. Using a properly prepared scrying mirror or bowl, see if you can locate the item.

Close the rite as usual.

If you could not find the item during the rite, on a second piece of parchment write the name of the item and the sigils of Azlyn and Leviathan. Place this beneath your mattress. Before you fall asleep, tell yourself you will find the item. See if you dream about the item.

    If neither of these produce results, wait one week. Usually within that time the item will be found or you'll remember where you left it.

## To Learn Magick

*Contributed by S.Connolly*

**Daemon Invoked:** Delepitore or similar Daemon

Oleum, Incense, Enns and Sigils of Delepitore

Within the ritual circle in honor of Delepitore:

Burn the sigil, wear the oleum, and request that she impart wisdom of sorcery and the arcane arts upon you.

Create a clay amulet of her sigil that you will wear or carry with you daily. You should feel heightened awareness. Answer to it.

# Demonolatry Rites

# To Infuse an Item with Specific Demonic Energy

*Contributed by S.Connolly*

You will need the following:
- An Item: Choose an item that you will infuse with a specific energy. For example - let's use money to illustrate the experiment - so we'll choose a wallet as our item.
- 2 Candles of corresponding color to the Demon and/or purpose of the item.
- Oleum of the Demon.
- Sigil of the Demon

We want to fill a wallet (the item in this instance), or even infuse it, with the energy of Belphegore (the Demon we've chosen).

To start, open ritual as usual, place two candles of color (corresponding to purpose) on your altar. In this case, we'll use GREEN candles.

Place the item (the Wallet in this example) on top of the sigil, between the candles.

Make sure you have the oleum of the demon whose energy you want to fill the item.

First, carve a one word statement being specific about what you want the item to contain on each candle. In this instance, we're going to write MONEY.

Then, anoint the candles with the Belphegore oleum (or oleum of your Demon of choice).

Now, during the rite imagine the energy of Belphegore as a green light eminating from the candles and the sigil and filling the wallet. Imagine the item sucking in the energy of Belphegore. Leave the item between the candles and on the sigil until the candles have burnt all the way down (you can use little candles for this - even votives). Then, burn the sigil. Take the ashes of the sigil and mix them with a few drops of the oleum. Anoint the item with the oleum. Take the ash mixture and put it in a small plastic bag or wrap them up in a small piece of cloth or piece of paper, and keep them in the wallet, or rub the ash all over the item.

Carry the item with you.

# APPENDICES I.
## The Nine Divinities and Their Considerations During Ritual

*Contributed by S. Connolly*

---

**Prayer Cords:** Prayer cords can be of any color and can be created with the Nine Divinities in any order you choose.

Traditionally the Demonic Divinities fall in the following order with regard to basic prayer cords:

1. Satan
2. Lucifer
3. Flereous
4. Leviathan
5. Belial
6. Unsere
7. Amducious
8. Verrine
9. Eurynomous

Satan is the first, then come the elementals from air to earth, then polarities of creation/destruction, and life/death. Verrine takes on the feminine aspect, as do both Lucifer and Leviathan in this instance. Unsere takes the feminine. Satan takes on no gender role. The rest are considered masculine.

## Invocation

When calling the demons into your ritual circle, the traditional way to do it is to use the enn, or an invocation of your own devise, and use the ritual dagger or your hand to draw the following in the air in front of you (kinda diagonal to the sky if that makes sense), starting at the arrow and ending at the dot:

It starts with the point closest to the arrow with Unsere, next is Lucifer, next is Flereous, next is Verrine, next is Belial, then Amducious, then Leviathan, Satan, and finally it ends at the dot with Eurynomous. It starts with creation, moves to enlightenment, and ends with destruction. It repeats this cycle three times. See **The Complete Book of Demonolatry** *by S. Connolly* for charts that break the demons down further.

## Diagrams of Ritual Layout

**Pyramid (triangle):** See the *Pyramid Rite* earlier in this book to see this diagram in function.

**Diagram of Altar Facing West**

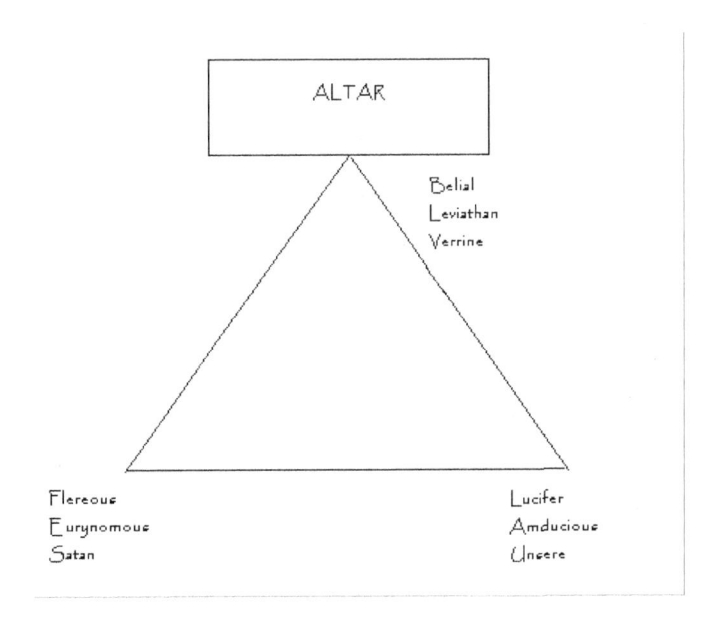

```
        ┌─────────────────┐
        │      ALTAR      │
        └────────┬────────┘
                /\
               /  \  Belial
              /    \ Leviathan
             /      \ Verrine
            /        \
           /          \
          /            \
         /              \
        /_____\
  Flereous              Lucifer
  Eurynomous            Amducious
  Satan                 Unsere
```

    This is not the only configuration that can be used. For example, all of the more "destructive" demons can be put together (Amducious, Flereous, Eurynomous), the creation demons put together (Unsere, Verrine, Leviathan), and all the the enlightenment demons put together (Lucifer, Belial, Satan).

## Circles using the nine (the top being Earth):

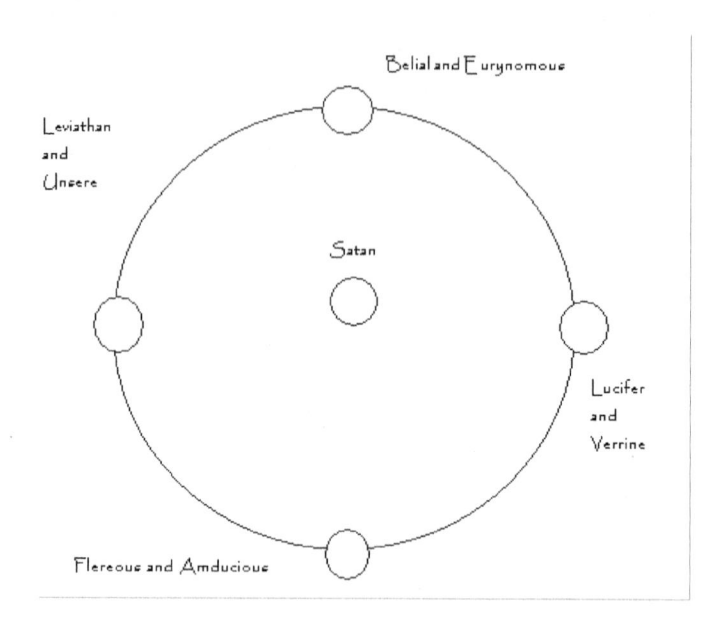

*Diagram of a circle with labels: Belial and Eurynomous (top), Leviathan and Unsere (upper left), Lucifer and Verrine (right), Flereous and Amducious (bottom), Satan (center).*

This particular circle is elemental. However, you can also choose polarity in which Lucifer and Leviathan would be in the East, Belial and Flereous in the North, Unsere and Amducious in the South, and Verrine and Eurynomous in the West. Or any combination thereof. In the case of Circles of Nine, Satan is always invoked from the center OR He can be invoked at every elemental point.

# APPENDICES
# II.
*Richard Dukante's Hierarchy*

While this information is readily available in **Lessons in Demonolatry** *by S. Connolly*, it is included here to make reference easier when creating your own rituals or when you need an enn quickly. This particular version of the hierarchy does not include descriptions of the demons from Ascension rites.

## Family 1

**Satan** - King : *Tasa reme laris Satan - Ave Satanis*

**Unsere** - Fertility and Sorcery : *Unsere tasa lirach on ca ayar*

**Satanchia** - Grand General (War) : *Furca na alle laris Satanchia*

**Agaliarept** - Assistant Grand General (War) : *On ca Agaliarept agna*

**Lucifage** - High Command (Control) : *Eyen tasa valocur Lucifuge Rofocale*

**Flereous** - Fire Elemental : *Ganic Tasa Fubin Flereous*

**Lucifer** - Air Elemental : *Renich Tasa Uberaca Biasa Icar Lucifer*

**Beelzebuth** - Lord of insects : *Adey vocar avage Beelzebuth*

**Belphegore** - Master of Weaponry- gain : *Lyan Ramec Catya Ganen Belphegore*

**Mesphito** - Keeper of the book of death : *Mesphito ramec viasa on ca*

**Delepitoré**- Demoness of magick. : *Deyen pretore ramec Delepitore on ca*

**Belial** - Earth Elemental : *Lirach Tasa Vefa Wehlc Belial*

## Family 2

**Luithian** - Advisor : *Deyan anay tasa Luithian*

**Leviathan** - Water Elemental : *Jaden Tasa Hoet Naca Leviathan*

**Sonnelion** - Demoness of hate : *Ayer Serpente Sonnillion*


## Family 3

**Abbadon** - Advisor : *Es na ayer Abbadon avage*

**Ammon** - demon of domination : *Avage Secore Ammon ninan*

**Mammon** - Demon of Avarice : *Tasa Mammon on ca lirach*

## Family 4

**Rosier** - Demon of love : *Serena Alora Rosier Aken*

**Astarte** - Demoness of love : *Serena Alora Astarte Aken*

**Ashtaroth** - Priestess of friendship : *Tasa Alora foren Ashtaroth*

**Astarot** - Matters concerning the heart : *Serena Alora Astartot Aken*

**Amducious** - The destroyer : *Denyen valocur avage secore Amducious*

**Asmodeus** - Demon of Lust : *Ayer avage Aloren Asmodeus aken*

## Family 5

**Eurynomous** - Demon of Death : *Ayar Secore on ca Eurynomous*

**Balberith** - Prince of dying : *Avage Secoré on ca Baalberith*

**Babeal** - Keeper of Graves : *Alan Secore on ca Babeal*

## Family 6

**Verrine** - Demon of Health : *Elan Typan Verrine*

**Verrier** - Demoness of herbal knowledge : *Elit Rayesta Verrier*

**Ronwe** - Demon of Knowledge : *Kaymen Vefa Ronwe*

## Family 7

**Svengali** - Demon of Vengeance : *Desa on Svengali ayer*

**Tezrian** - Priestess of battle : *Ezyr ramec ganen Tezrian*

## Family 8

**Asafoetida** - Demoness of feminine attributes: *Asana nanay on ca Asafoetida*

**Rashoon** - Priestess of seduction: *Taran Rashoon nanay*

**Taroon** - Priestess of Desire: *Taroon an ca nanay*

## **Family 9**

Consists of lesser hierarchy

**Berith**: *Hoath redar ganabal Berith*

**Agares**: *Rean ganen ayar da Agares*

**Abigor**: *Aylan Abigor tasa uan on ca*

**Lillith**: *Renich viasa avage lillith lirach*

## NOTES

## NOTES

## NOTES

## NOTES

More Titles Available From...
# DB PUBLISHING

## S. Connolly:
- *The Complete Book of Demonolatry*
- *The Art of Creative Magick*

## Ellen Purswell:
- *Goetic Demonolatry*

## Various Authors
- *Demonolatry Rites*

## Journals and Calendars
- *The Meditation Journal*
- *Ritus Record Libri*
- *Diabolus Atrum Iter Itineris*

## Music:
- *Abyss: Daemonolatry Hymns for Ritual & Meditation*

*Purchase our titles at:*
http://www.lulu.com/demonolatry/

*Books For Demonolators By Demonolators* TM

**Demonolatry Rites**

**Demonolatry Rites**

**Demonolatry Rites**

Printed in Great Britain
by Amazon